Pray

Pray is the ideal reboot for a flagging devotional life. It is warm and biblical and practical. I will be recommending it to lots of people.
Julian Hardyman, Senior Pastor at Eden Baptist Church, Cambridge and author of Idols, Maximum Life and Fresh Pathways in Prayer

A helpful resource which enables you to feed on God's Word and be urged on to pray. There are many lessons here from the prayers of God's people in both the Old and New Testaments, as well as Jesus' prayers for the church. What a great way to spend a month, studying prayer with such a wide range of applications, alongside the encouragement to pray more ourselves!
Karen Soole, Women's Worker at Trinity Church, Lancaster and Chair of the Northern Women's Convention

30-DAY DEVOTIONAL

Pray

Edited by Elizabeth McQuoid

FOOD
FOR THE
JOURNEY

INTER-VARSITY PRESS
36 Causton Street, London SW1P 4ST, England
Email: ivp@ivpbooks.com
Website: www.ivpbooks.com

First published 2020

British Library Cataloguing-in-Publication Data
A catalogue record for this book is available from the British Library.

ISBN: 978–1–78974–169–8
eBook ISBN: 978–1–78974–170–4

Set in Avenir 11/15pt
Typeset in Great Britain by CRB Associates, Potterhanworth, Lincolnshire
Printed in Great Britain by Ashford Colour Press Ltd, Gosport, Hampshire

Contributors

Nehemiah 1 and Habakkuk 1 and 3
Jonathan Lamb

Jonathan is Minister-at-Large for Keswick Ministries. He previously served as CEO of Keswick Ministries and Director of Langham Preaching. He is the author of a number of books, including *Preaching Matters* and *Essentially One.* He is also a Vice President of International Fellowship of Evangelical Students (IFES).

Psalm 51
David Coffey

David was the General Secretary of the Baptist Union of Great Britain for fifteen years. He then became President of the Baptist World Alliance and is now the Global Ambassador for BMS World Mission.

Daniel 6
Alistair Begg

Alistair has been the Senior Pastor at Parkside Church, Ohio, USA since 1983. He has written a number of books, including *Pray Big*. A popular conference speaker, he is also the voice behind the daily radio broadcast, *Truth for Life*.

Luke 22
Raymond Brown
Formerly Principal of Spurgeon's College in London, Raymond has also worked as a Baptist minister in Cambridge and Torquay. He is the author of a number of books, including several volumes in IVP's The Bible Speaks Today series.

John 17
Bruce Milne
Until 2001, Bruce was Pastor of First Baptist Church in Vancouver, Canada. Previously, he taught at Spurgeon's College, London. He is the author of *Know the Truth*, *Dynamic Diversity* and The Bible Speaks Today volume, *The Message of John*.

Ephesians 1
Rico Tice
Rico is Senior Minister (Evangelism) at All Souls Church, Langham Place in London. He is the co-founder of Christianity Explored Ministries. He has written a number of books, including *Honest Evangelism* and *Capturing God*.

Ephesians 6
Calisto Odede

Calisto is Senior Pastor of Nairobi Pentecostal Church, Kenya. Previously, he served with the Fellowship of Christian Unions (FOCUS) and with the International Fellowship of Evangelical Students (IFES).

Philippians 1 and 1 Thessalonians 3
Paul Mallard

Paul is Senior Pastor of Widcombe Baptist Church in Bath. He has served as the President of the Fellowship of Independent Evangelical Churches (FIEC) and is the author of *Invest Your Suffering*, *Invest Your Disappointments*, *Staying Fresh* and *An Identity to Die For.*

James 1 and 5
Michael Baughen

Michael was Rector of Holy Trinity Church, Platt Lane in Rusholme, Manchester, and at All Souls, Langham Place, London, before becoming Bishop of Chester. Following his retirement, he worked as an honorary assistant bishop in the dioceses of London and Southwark. He is also a hymn writer.

Preface

What is the collective name for a group of preachers? A troop, a gaggle, a chatter, a pod . . . ? I'm not sure! But in this Food for the Journey series we have gathered an excellent group of Bible teachers to help us to unpack the Scriptures and understand some of the core issues that every Christian needs to know and understand.

Each book is based on a particular theme and contains excerpts from messages by much-loved Keswick Convention speakers, past and present. When necessary, the language has been updated but, on the whole, this is what you would have heard had you been listening in the tent on Skiddaw Street. A wide, though not exhaustive, selection of Bible passages explores the key theme, and each day of the devotional ends with a fresh section on how to apply God's Word to your own life and situation.

Whether you are a Convention regular or have never been to Keswick, this Food for the Journey series provides a unique opportunity to study the Scriptures and a particular topic with a range of gifted Bible teachers by your side. Each book is designed to fit in your jacket pocket, rucksack or handbag, so you can read it anywhere – over the breakfast table, on the commute into work or college, while you are waiting in your car, during your lunch break or in bed at night. Wherever life's journey takes you, time in God's Word is vital nourishment for your spiritual journey.

Our prayer is that these devotionals become your daily feast, a nourishing opportunity to meet with God through his Word. Read, meditate on, apply, and pray through the Scriptures selected for each day, and allow God's truths to take deep root and transform your life.

If these devotionals whet your appetite for more, there is a 'For further study' section at the end of each book. You can also visit our website <www.keswickministries.org> to find the full range of books, study guides, CDs, DVDs and mp3s available.

> *Let the word of Christ dwell in you richly.*
> (Colossians 3:16, ESV)

Introduction
Prayer works

In the 1950s, Dorothea Clapp began to pray faithfully for the students in her local high school in New Jersey, USA. She asked God to touch the world through the lives of those young people. She gave a copy of John's Gospel to one of those students, a young man who would later become a Christian at a Billy Graham meeting. That young man was George Verwer, the founder of Operation Mobilization, a global mission organization that now serves in 110 countries and sails to many others with the ministry ship MV *Logos Hope.* His life has indeed touched the world.

As Dorothea and countless others have found, prayer works. So why are we so reluctant to pray? Perhaps because prayer is hard work. We constantly have to call our wandering hearts and minds to attention. Perhaps because we're riddled with despair and doubt when God doesn't seem to answer our prayers. Perhaps because it seems such a passive thing to do when action is required elsewhere.

Yet, despite our meagre efforts and frequent failure, the Bible relentlessly calls us to pray. It gives us examples of people praying – for children, enemies, nations, forgiveness and healing – both publicly and privately. Matthew 6:5–15 gives us 'Prayer 101', describing how we should pray, and citing the most famous prayer in the world: 'Our Father in Heaven . . .' It is significant that the only tutorial the disciples asked for was on the very subject of prayer. God wants us to succeed in this endeavour, so much so that when we are struggling to know what to pray, he promises that the Holy Spirit will groan on our behalf, bringing our requests to the Father (Romans 8:26).

To encourage us to see the power of prayer and to pray expectantly and persistently, the Bible even gives us a glimpse of what happens when our prayers reach God's throne room. So often we worry that God doesn't hear our prayers. Yet Revelation 8:3–5 tells us that an angel stands at the altar with a golden censer offering our prayers mixed with incense to God. Our prayers come before him and then are combined with fire from the altar and hurled back down to earth. The result is 'peals of thunder, rumblings, flashes of lightning and an earthquake' (Revelation 8:5). 'Prayer doesn't frequently bring with it the sensation of cosmic power unleashed, what poet George Herbert called "reversed thunder." But that is exactly what is happening! The whole creation is shaken by the prayers of the saints. Something is happening as they pray. Work is being done, whether they see it or not' (Ben Patterson, *Deepening Your Conversation with God*, Baker, 2001, pp. 24–25). Prayer is powerful, not because of our words but because God is powerful, and he uses it as a means of accomplishing his work in the world.

Prayer also changes us. It is the best kind of virtuous circle. The more we pray, the more we realize we need to pray; we see the power of prayer and our relationship with God deepens. We increasingly appreciate the access Jesus' death on the cross gives us into the very throne room of God, and we're keen to make the most of the privilege. Prayer becomes less of a 'have to' and more of a 'want to'. It becomes less about meeting my needs and more about meeting God. It becomes less about presenting my shopping list of requests and more about conforming my will to God's. It becomes a regular, holy opportunity to say, like Jesus, 'Not my will, but yours, be done.'

Most of us feel like novices when it comes to praying. Don Carson likens us to 'nasty little boys who ring front door bells and run away before anyone answers' (*A Call to Spiritual Reformation*, IVP, 2011, p. 37). We need to learn to pray deeper, longer, more fervent prayers. Or, as the Puritans used to say, we need to 'pray until we pray'. The Bible urges us to devote ourselves to prayer (Colossians 4:2) and to 'pray continually' (1 Thessalonians 5:17).

This devotional will help to kick-start the process. These thirty days will take us on a whistle-stop tour of the Bible. We'll look at the Psalms, the prayer book of the Bible, which models, among other things, repentance and lament for us. We'll look in the Gospels to see what Jesus prayed and to learn his priorities. We'll join with the apostle Paul to pray for the church and for our own spiritual growth. We'll cry out with the prophet Habakkuk when God seems far away and doesn't answer our prayers as we'd hoped. Nehemiah will teach us how to pray for our nation and James how to pray for the sick. No one book could ever exhaust the subject of prayer – indeed, whole libraries are full of books on prayer – but our brief tour will provide examples to follow and words to pray.

When Dorothea Clapp started praying, she could never have imagined how God would answer her prayers and touch lives far beyond her expectations. Neither can we. But we can be certain of one thing: we can't afford not to pray. Which is why the book in your hands could be life-transforming.

Now to him who is able to do immeasurably more than all we ask or imagine, according to his power that is at work within us, to him be glory in the church and in Christ Jesus throughout all generations, for ever and ever! Amen. (Ephesians 3:20–21)

Nehemiah

King Cyrus of Persia had allowed the Jewish exiles to return to Jerusalem. But when Nehemiah, cupbearer to King Artaxerxes, heard almost a hundred years later that the city walls of his homeland had not been rebuilt, he was heartbroken. The king allowed him to return to oversee the building project. The book of Nehemiah recounts the rebuilding of the wall, the opposition the Jewish people encountered, the residents chosen to live in the city, the spiritual revival when Ezra read God's law and Nehemiah's reforms. It also records a selection of Nehemiah's prayers, which model for us how we can turn to God in any and every situation.

Day 1

Read: Nehemiah 1:1–11
Key verses: Nehemiah 1:4–6

....

⁴For some days I mourned and fasted and prayed before the God of heaven. ⁵Then I said:

'LORD, the God of heaven, the great and awesome God, who keeps his covenant of love with those who love him and keep his commandments, ⁶let your ear be attentive . . . to hear the prayer your servant is praying . . . for your servants, the people of Israel.'

'Why pray when you can worry?' seems to be the maxim of our day. In contrast, when he heard about the devastation in Jerusalem, Nehemiah committed himself to weeks of prayer. There was nothing else he could do – no-one but God could accomplish what needed to be done.

One great value in facing desperate situations is that we are forced to hold fast to God. 'I have been driven many times to my knees by the overwhelming conviction that I had nowhere else to go. My own wisdom and that of those about me seemed insufficient for the day' are words attributed to Abraham Lincoln. That is how Nehemiah felt, and that is the attitude we need to cultivate throughout the Christian life, especially in our praying.

Verse 5 introduces us to a model of how to pray in a desperate situation. 'Lord, the God of heaven' is always the right place to begin. Nehemiah cries out to the Lord, Yahweh, the personal God, the God of the exodus who had saved his people (verse 10) and defeated their enemies. He prays to the God of heaven, the Sovereign Lord who has universal supremacy, the transcendent Creator, the God above all others, who has the power to fulfil his purposes (see 2:4, 20; 4:14; 9:32).

For Nehemiah, this was neither theoretical nor formal. He refers to the great and awesome God as 'my God' – a phrase that appears ten times in his memoirs. In the building programme he was to lead, in the opposition he was to confront and in the reforms he was to introduce, he would depend on 'my God' at every turn. Like Moses, 'he persevered because he saw him who is invisible' (Hebrews 11:27).

Some of us serve God in places where the human and financial resources are minuscule, and where the temptation to give up is a daily one. In such circumstances, we need to be able to 'see' the Lord, Yahweh, the God of heaven. It certainly makes a difference to the way we pray if, first of all, we raise our eyes to 'the God of heaven, the great and awesome God'.

Fast-forward to the New Testament and a prison cell . . . Peter and John had just spent a night in jail, persecution was set to increase, and yet, when the believers prayed, their first words were: 'Sovereign Lord . . . you made the heaven and the earth and the sea, and everything in them' (Acts 4:24). Their focus, like Nehemiah's, was not on the magnitude of the task but on the magnitude of their God. Whatever you have to deal with today, will you begin your prayers by acknowledging the sovereignty of God and your dependence on the 'Lord, the God of heaven'?

Day 2

Read: Nehemiah 1:1–11
Key verses: Nehemiah 1:5–7

....

⁵*Then I said:*

> *'Lᴏʀᴅ, the God of heaven, the great and awesome God, who keeps his covenant of love with those who love him and keep his commandments, ⁶let your ear be attentive and your eyes open to hear the prayer your servant is praying . . . I confess the sins we Israelites, including myself and my father's family, have committed against you. ⁷We have acted very wickedly towards you. We have not obeyed the commands, decrees and laws you gave your servant Moses.*

It is never easy to say sorry. But, as he entered God's presence, Nehemiah knew it was vital to repent before God.

The judgment of God, which had resulted in the destruction of Jerusalem, was a result of the Israelites' sin. So it followed that, if Nehemiah was about to appeal to God for the restoration of the city and its people, it would have to be done on the basis of confession of those very sins that had led to its destruction.

Nehemiah doesn't distance himself from the people, but identifies with them and acknowledges his own sinfulness before God. There is nothing self-righteous or superior about him. Similarly, on discovering the unfaithfulness of the people, Ezra had prayed, 'I am too ashamed and disgraced, my God, to lift up my face to you, because our sins are higher than our heads and our guilt has reached to the heavens' (Ezra 9:6). This kind of solidarity is important. It is all too easy to criticize the church or distance ourselves from its failings, but when the Holy Spirit is at work, he will show us that we too are guilty.

Mourning over the state of our church and our country is one of the lessons of this chapter; coming in confession to a holy God is an essential part of that process. Nehemiah would know God's blessing only as he and the people expressed genuine repentance for their unfaithfulness. One of the recurring features of revival – those significant times of spiritual renewal and awakening among God's people – is this awareness of the awfulness of sin and a willingness to confront it in prayerful repentance. As we confront the challenges of God's Word and allow the Holy Spirit to review our attitudes, our behaviour, our habits, our motivations and our priorities, we too will begin to see sin as God sees it and pray as Nehemiah did.

Today, repent before God for the sins of our nation, using some words from Daniel:

Lord, the great and awesome God, who keeps his covenant of love with those who love him and keep his commandments, we have sinned and done wrong. We have been wicked and have rebelled; we have turned away from your commands and laws . . . Lord, you are righteous, but this day we are covered with shame . . . because we have sinned against you . . . Lord, in keeping with all your righteous acts, turn away your anger and your wrath . . . hear the prayers and petitions of your servant . . . We do not make requests of you because we are righteous, but because of your great mercy. Lord, listen! Lord, forgive! Lord, hear and act! For your sake, my God, do not delay.
(Daniel 9:4, 8, 16, 17, 18–19)

Day 3

Read: Nehemiah 1:1–11
Key verses: Nehemiah 1:8–9

....

> [8]*Remember the instruction you gave your servant Moses, saying, 'If you are unfaithful, I will scatter you among the nations,* [9]*but if you return to me and obey my commands, then even if your exiled people are at the farthest horizon, I will gather them from there and bring them to the place I have chosen as a dwelling for my Name.'*

Often, we feel unable to pray because we are paralysed by a sense of our failure. We can't imagine that God would listen to us, let alone accept us back. It is then we return to the truth that, however tenuous our hold of him might seem, God will never let us go: he 'keeps his covenant of love' (verse 5).

One of the most distinctive ideas in the Old Testament is God's steady persistence in loving his people despite their extraordinary waywardness. That's what he promised, and he will remain faithful to that promise. The Bible uses the word 'covenant' (which we saw yesterday and the day before) to describe that relationship, and Nehemiah's prayer is based on that foundation: God can be trusted. God's covenants in the Old Testament were founded on his sovereign grace. He had chosen the Jews, revealed himself to them and rescued them – so he would never give up on them. That's why Nehemiah prays, 'Remember.' It is a key word in the book of Nehemiah (4:14; 5:19; 6:14; 13:14, 22, 29, 31) and it represents a call for God to intervene. Nehemiah is saying, 'If you have been faithful to your promise in sending us into exile because of our sinfulness, now – as we obey you – fulfil your promise to bring us back and restore us.' The same theme comes through in the prayer of chapter 9, which is saturated with that kind of covenant language – *your* people, *our* God, *my* God. Nehemiah prays: we belong to you, so please be faithful in fulfilling your covenant promise.

Of course, the greatest covenant of all is found in Jesus Christ. By faith in him, we have been brought into a covenant relationship with the living God and with his global family, founded on God's grace. So, when we pray, however inadequately, it is on the basis of God's having chosen us, having welcomed us into his family and having saved us through Christ's work. Like Nehemiah, we can appeal to the Lord: 'We belong to you, please don't give up on us but be faithful in keeping your promises.' Whatever our emotional or spiritual state, we can come to God knowing that his grace never ends. He is the faithful God who keeps his promises.

Shortly before he was assassinated, the deputy governor of the Maze prison in Northern Ireland, William McConnell, said,

> I have committed my life, talents, work and action to Almighty God, in the sure and certain knowledge that, however slight my hold of him may have been, his promises are sure and his hold on me complete.
>
> (Jonathan Lamb, *From Why to Worship*, Authentic Media, 2007, p. 53)

Today, come to God in prayer, knowing that you belong to him and that, despite your faithlessness, he remains faithful and will always keep his promises.

Psalms

Imagine being able to sing the songs Jesus sang or pray the prayers he prayed. Well, you can! Jesus, like many Israelites before and after him, used psalms in public and private worship. The book of Psalms is a collection of prayers and songs gathered over a number of centuries and written by a variety of authors, including King David. The Psalms are full of personal testimony but also direct our focus to God as King and Creator, Judge and Redeemer, Helper and Deliverer. Each psalm is carefully crafted poetry, rich in imagery and, although written for a specific context, contains timeless truths. On any and every occasion, we can go to the Psalms to find words to express our emotions and words of Scripture to speak to God.

Day 4

Read: Psalm 51

Key verses: Psalm 51:1–2

....

¹Have mercy on me, O God,
*   according to your unfailing love;*
according to your great compassion
*   blot out my transgressions.*
²Wash away all my iniquity
*   and cleanse me from my sin.*

Psalm 51 is a prayer of repentance, modelling the way back to God when we have sinned. David wrote this psalm at a tragic time in his life, after Nathan the prophet confronted him over his adultery with Bathsheba and his murder of her husband, Uriah (2 Samuel 11 – 12). But this psalm is not just for murderers and adulterers, although it is certainly for them; it is for all who seek to regain the peace and presence of God that they have lost through sinning. Thousands of sinners have found their way back to God, long after they had given up hope, through the words of this psalm.

Where does this journey start?

• By remembering you belong to God

For all his wretchedness, David knows that he still belongs to God and therefore he appeals to God's unfailing love (verse 1). God has made a commitment between himself and his people; although David has broken his part of the agreement, he still appeals to the mercy, grace and compassion of his covenant-keeping God.

• By recognizing your sin for what it is

David cries out to God to 'blot out my transgressions'. He knows he has a record that needs to be cleared. 'Transgressions' carries the idea of a revolt, of self-assertion. David is asking God to 'blot out' his rebellion. In verse 2, he says, 'Wash away all my iniquity.' Iniquity implies waywardness, a deliberate choosing of the wrong path. David asks God to wash him – a gentle rinse will not do; he needs to be thoroughly scrubbed because this waywardness has gone so deep. He knows he needs to be cleansed from his sin – his own failures and faults for which he cannot blame anyone else.

David was constantly aware of his sin (verse 3). He realized it was primarily an offence against God (verse 4) and that it had pervaded his existence from the beginning (verse 5). He admits that he knew God's plan for righteous living but chose to go his own way instead.

When Nathan the prophet confronted David with his sin, he declared bluntly, 'You are the man!' (2 Samuel 12:7). Invite the Holy Spirit to search your heart and, when he confronts you with your sin, respond humbly like David and say to the Lord, 'You [are] justified in your words and blameless in your judgement' (Psalm 51:4, ESV).

Begin the journey of repentance today by confessing your sins before God:

Heavenly Father, I'm sorry for _____. I know my sin is an offence to you because you are pure and holy. Please forgive me for turning away from you and your Word. Thank you that though I am faithless, you remain faithful to me and to all your promises. Thank you for your unfailing love and mercy and that I am yours – now and for evermore. Help me today to live as your child, for your pleasure and glory. Amen.

Day 5

Read: Psalm 51
Key verses: Psalm 51:7–9

••

> *7Cleanse me with hyssop, and I shall be clean;*
>   *wash me, and I shall be whiter than snow.*
> *8Let me hear joy and gladness;*
>   *let the bones you have crushed rejoice.*
> *9Hide your face from my sins*
>   *and blot out all my iniquity.*

What's next? When we have agreed with God about the severity of our sin, what happens next in this journey towards repentance?

David asks God to apply his cure: 'Cleanse me, wash me, speak to me, hide your face from my sin and blot out my record.' The cure in David's day was a branch of hyssop dipped in sacrificial blood and applied to the person concerned – then came the pronouncement: 'You are clean' (see Leviticus 14:1–7; Hebrews 9:19–22). David didn't want to hear: 'You are the man!' Rather, he wanted to hear the words: 'You are clean.'

Jeremiah talks about people discovering that soap and detergent will not touch the stain that is in them (Jeremiah 2:22). But Jesus' death on the cross would provide that once-and-for-all blood sacrifice for sin. 'If we confess our sins, he is faithful and just and will forgive us our sins and purify us from all unrighteousness' (1 John 1:9). Jesus says the words we need to hear: 'You are clean.' 'As far as the east is from the west, so far has he removed our transgressions from us' (Psalm 103:12).

From verse 10 onwards, the prayer is no longer focused on dealing negatively with sin. David is asking God to perform his miracle: 'Create in me a pure heart.' The word 'create' is only ever used in connection with God's work. This is something that human beings can never do for themselves. Today, we can read verses 10–12 as New Testament Christians. Thank God that the work of creating a new heart in the believer has happened: 'If the Spirit of him who raised Jesus from the dead is living in you, he who raised Christ from the dead will also give life to your mortal bodies because of his Spirit who lives in you' (Romans 8:11). This work of the Holy Spirit, begun on earth, will be completed in the new creation when Christ returns as King.

What are the results of this kind of prayer? Our new hearts will be full of praise, thanksgiving (verses 14–15) and meaningful worship (verses 16–17). Personal repentance will lead to corporate blessings (verses 18–19). Just as sin can spoil a family, church and nation, repentance and forgiveness can bless a family, church and nation. And there is a restored ministry, a second chance for fruitful service (verse 13). Who else better to lead other sinners back to God than a repentant prodigal?

There's a way back to God
from the dark paths of sin;
there's a door that is open
and you may go in:
at Calvary's cross
is where you begin,
when you come as a sinner to Jesus.
(E. H. Swinstead, 1882–1950)

Today, come to the cross. Ask God for his cleansing and forgiveness. Invite the Holy Spirit to do his work in your heart – renewing your love for God, reviving your worship, restoring you to fruitful service and making you a blessing to others.

Daniel

Daniel was one of the young Jewish men carried off into exile in Babylon by King Nebuchadnezzar. He was given a job in the palace, and his work ethic and integrity meant he quickly rose through the ranks to become one of the king's most trusted servants. His book is made up of historical narrative (chapters 1 – 6) and highly symbolic prophetic visions (chapters 7 – 12); it reveals Daniel to be an interpreter of dreams and a man who cultivated the habit of prayer. God's sovereignty is a key theme: 'the Most High God is sovereign over all kingdoms on earth' (5:21).

Day 6

Read: Daniel 6:1–28
Key verse: Daniel 6:10

....

Now when Daniel learned that the decree had been published, he went home to his upstairs room where the windows opened towards Jerusalem. Three times a day he got down on his knees and prayed, giving thanks to his God, just as he had done before.

It was the perfect trap.

'All [have] agreed that the king should issue an edict and enforce the decree that anyone who prays to any god or human being during the next thirty days, except to you, Your Majesty, shall be thrown into the lions' den' (Daniel 6:7). The 120 satraps who ruled Babylon couldn't find anything with which to discredit Daniel before King Darius. The only way they could topple Daniel from power was to use his faith against him.

But, despite the king's edict, Daniel kept on praying as he had always done (verse 13). This wasn't an act of defiance but a display of discipline. It was this unswerving discipline that made it possible for his colleagues to catch him in the act. In his daily regime of prayer, with his face towards Jerusalem, Daniel displayed to all who knew him his belief that salvation was to be found only in the God of Israel. If his prayer had been a triviality to him and his colleagues, no-one would have cared about it. But his prayer was symbolic of the deep-rooted conviction of his life concerning God and his desire to serve him.

When crises hit our lives – the loss of a job, bereavement, a relationship falling apart – there is a sense in which they do something in us: they forge character for the future. But they reveal more than they create. The crisis of Darius' edict did not make Daniel a man of prayer: it revealed him to be a man of prayer.

Daniel had made the habit of prayer such an integral part of his life that the momentum sustained him. Some days, he might have been excited or inspired; other days, a little bored, but he always prayed. It was his custom. Daniel knew the race of life was not a sprint but a cross-country run, and his steady disciplined commitment highlights the priority of developing holy habits. In the New Testament, we read how Jesus went up to the synagogue on the

Sabbath 'as was his custom' (Luke 4:16). Jesus himself established holy habits. Some object, saying, 'But that is just legalism.' How is it that when you are doing physical exercises, it's liberation, but when you are doing spiritual exercises, it's legalism?

Are you cultivating the holy habit of prayer?

> We don't drift into spiritual life; we do not drift into disciplined prayer. We do not grow in prayer unless we plan to pray. That means we must set aside time to do nothing but pray. What we actually do reflects our highest priorities. That means that we can proclaim our commitment to prayer until the cows come home, but unless we actually pray, our actions disown our words.
>
> (D. A. Carson, *A Call to Spiritual Reformation*, IVP, 2011, p. 19)

Habakkuk

We don't often get an insight into a prophet's private prayer life. In the book of Habakkuk, however, we see the prophet crying out to God. Habakkuk was a contemporary of Jeremiah and lived in Jerusalem. Under King Jehoiakim, wickedness, violence and anarchy were rife, and the prophet could not understand why God did not intervene. When God finally answered his prayer and told him judgment would come through the hands of the evil Babylonians, Habakkuk was even more perplexed. So we should ask: what changed the questions of 'Why?' and 'How long, LORD?' in chapter 1 to the worship of chapter 3? When God doesn't answer our prayers as we had hoped, when we don't understand what he is doing, how can we say, as Habakkuk finally did, 'Yet I will rejoice in the LORD, I will be joyful in God my Saviour' (3:18)?

Day 7

Read: Habakkuk 1

Key verses: Habakkuk 1:2–3

....

> [2]*How long, LORD, must I call for help,*
>   *but you do not listen?*
> *Or cry out to you, 'Violence!'*
>   *but you do not save?*
> [3]*Why do you make me look at injustice?*
>   *Why do you tolerate wrongdoing?*
> *Destruction and violence are before me;*
>   *there is strife, and conflict abounds.*

Why? How long?

Do your prayers start like this? The prophet Habakkuk was overwhelmed by these questions. He was living in Jerusalem during the reign of King Jehoiakim, who reversed all the good work which his father Josiah had achieved. During Jehoiakim's reign, the people ignored God's laws, so moral and terrible spiritual decline set in. The priests, politicians and civil servants took their cue from the king and they too became perpetrators of violence and injustice, adding to the moral confusion rather than resolving it. Habakkuk concluded, 'The wicked hem in the righteous' (verse 4). The few who did remain faithful to God were completely surrounded by ungodly behaviour that threatened to snuff out all signs of spiritual life.

Habakkuk not only wrestled with the situation, he wrestled with God. There is an intensity to verses 2–3. They imply that Habakkuk shouted, screamed, 'Help, Lord! Why are you allowing people to drift away? Why are you not intervening?' The real crisis for Habakkuk was not simply the appalling deterioration he witnessed among God's people. The crisis was compounded by the fact that he petitioned again and again, but it seemed that God was not listening. Habakkuk was bewildered and cried out to God in pain. As the novelist Peter de Vries puts it, the question mark is 'twisted like a fish hook in the human heart' (*The Blood of the Lamb*, University of Chicago Press, 2005, p. 243).

It is very important that we follow Habakkuk's example and admit our bewilderment at the perplexing questions and mysteries of life. We must pray honestly. 'We need not attempt to bottle it up, because God invites us to pour it out' (John Goldingay, *God's Prophet, God's Servant*, Paternoster Press, 1984, p. 29). It is false spirituality to imagine that we must not ask these questions. If we try to exhibit a brave and cheerful face before other Christians or even before God, when inwardly we feel torn apart, it is almost certain to accentuate our distress. It is a mark of mature spirituality to confess these things to God.

Why, LORD, do you stand far off?
    Why do you hide yourself in times of trouble?
(Psalm 10:1)

My soul is in deep anguish.
    How long, LORD, how long?
(Psalm 6:3)

Join Habakkuk, the psalmist and believers down through the centuries as you bring your own situation before God and cry out 'Why?' and 'How long?' Admit your bewilderment and lay out your complaint honestly before him. Don't be tempted to believe Satan's lie that God's apparent silence means that he is neither interested nor working on your behalf. Ask God to help you trust his character, and learn to live with unanswered questions and mystery.

Day 8

Read: Habakkuk 1
Key verses: Habakkuk 1:5–6

....

> ⁵*Look at the nations and watch –*
> *and be utterly amazed.*
> *For I am going to do something in your days*
> *that you would not believe,*
> *even if you were told.*
> ⁶*I am raising up the Babylonians,*
> *that ruthless and impetuous people,*
> *who sweep across the whole earth*
> *to seize dwellings not their own.*

When we pray, we usually have in mind exactly how we would like God to answer our prayer. Habakkuk certainly did. But God told him to 'look' (verse 5), which picks up Habakkuk's complaint in verse 3: 'Why do you make me look at injustice?' God encourages Habakkuk to take a wider look, to gain a divine perspective, and see that

God is working in ways 'you would not believe, even if you were told'.

God's solution to the problem which so concerned Habakkuk was to send the Babylonians to bring devastation on the Israelites. The Babylonians were guilty of international terrorism, ethnic cleansing and the exercise of ruthless power. What was so troubling for Habakkuk was that, although the Babylonians were in the driving seat of this great war machine, God was the Commander. Why was God doing this? It was part of disciplining his people. They had ignored his justice, so Babylonian justice was what they would receive. If God's people were guilty of perpetrating violence and destruction, violence was what they would have.

The Babylonians were not just under God's sovereign authority, they were an instrument for God's purposes. This is because God is the God of history, in control of the movements even of pagan nations. It might have seemed that it was the military prowess of the Babylonians that would eventually result in their success, but it was God who had raised them up to fulfil his purpose.

Exactly the same truth is found in the New Testament. The early Christians were bewildered at what had happened when Jesus was crucified. In their prayer meeting, they stated that Herod, Pontius Pilate, the Gentiles and the people of Israel had conspired against Jesus. But then they added, 'They did what your power and will decided beforehand should happen' (Acts 4:28). They realized that the apparently disastrous events in Jerusalem when Jesus was crucified were not completely out of control. There was another story. It was all to do with God's power, his will and his decision.

If God is not answering your prayers as you'd hoped, will you ask him to help you to look at your situation with fresh eyes? Pray that you will be able to see the ways in which he is working, acknowledge his control and trust his good purposes.

When we don't receive what we pray for or desire, it doesn't mean that God isn't acting on our behalf. Rather, he's weaving his story. Paul tells us to 'continue steadfastly in prayer, being watchful in it with thanksgiving' (Colossians 4:2). Thanksgiving helps us be grace-centred, seeing all of life as a gift. It looks at how God's past blessings impact our lives. Watchfulness alerts us to the unfolding drama in the present. It looks for God's present working as it unfolds into future grace.
(Paul E. Miller, *A Praying Life*, NavPress, 2009, p. 187)

Day 9

Read: Habakkuk 1
Key verses: Habakkuk 1:12–13

••

¹²LORD, are you not from everlasting?
  My God, my Holy One, you will never die.
You, LORD, have appointed them to execute
    judgment;
  you, my Rock, have ordained them to punish.
¹³Your eyes are too pure to look on evil;
  you cannot tolerate wrongdoing.
Why then do you tolerate the treacherous?
  Why are you silent while the wicked
  swallow up those more righteous than
    themselves?

Habakkuk could hardly believe his ears. As a prophet, he knew that judgment on the Israelites was inevitable. But he couldn't understand how, if God was meant to be the God of awesome purity, he could allow the ruthless Babylonians to do their worst (verse 13). The suspicion was that 'if God uses them, he must be like them'. The imagery of verses 14–17 underlines the ruthless behaviour of the Babylonians. Like a fisherman with rod and net, they sat beside the stream that God had generously stocked with human fish: 'he gathers them up in his drag-net; and so he rejoices and is glad' (verse 15). Habakkuk was appalled by the brutality. He wondered how it could possibly fulfil God's purposes and how long it would last.

But like many of the psalmists and other prophets, Habakkuk set his questions in the context of his certainties. In the midst of his perplexity, he affirmed what he knew to be true about God's character and purpose (verse 12). He expressed confidence in three things: God's commitment, God's eternity and God's purpose.

• God's commitment

   He spoke to God in direct and personal terms: 'My God, my Holy One'. He was implying, 'You are the faithful, covenant-keeping God. I belong to you.' This is our confidence too. God will not let go of us. Whatever happens, we belong to him. This security is not dependent on the strength of our faith but on God's faithful commitment to us.

- God's eternity

  'LORD, are you not from everlasting?' God is not only engaged in history, but he is also above all its turbulent ebb and flow. Whatever our fears and uncertainties, God is eternal, the Rock, the one stable element in an uncertain world. If things are shaking in our lives or in our world, we must hold on to God's changelessness.

- God's purpose

  Habakkuk realized that the coming Babylonian invasion was something that God had ordained. Other prophets, such as Ezekiel, Jeremiah and Isaiah, also realized that international events are not random but are all part of God's sovereign purpose. 'You, LORD, have appointed them . . .' (verse 12).

When we are in difficult situations, it is very easy for questions and doubts to overwhelm us. We need to remind ourselves of the certainties of God's Word and repeat to ourselves the confident realities expressed in these verses. If we respond in prayer as Habakkuk did – even in the blackest moments of our lives – we will discover that God is our refuge and strength.

Never doubt in the dark what God has told you in the light.

(Warren Wiersbe, *Be Comforted*, David C. Cook Publishing, 2009, p. 148)

When your heart is breaking with unanswered questions, rehearse the certainties of God's Word, the rock-solid truths of the Christian faith. Pray these truths of Scripture back to God, speak them to your own soul. Cling to God in dependence and trust. Acknowledge that, regardless of the circumstances, he is *your* Lord, *your* Holy One, *your* Rock (see Habakkuk 1:12).

Day 10

Read: Habakkuk 3
Key verse: Habakkuk 3:2

•••

> LORD, I have heard of your fame;
>   I stand in awe of your deeds, LORD.
> Repeat them in our day,
>   in our time make them known;
>   in wrath remember mercy.

Sometimes we struggle to know how to pray for our community and nation. The needs are overwhelming, as is the sinfulness all around us. Chapter 3 provides us with a model prayer. Notice three things about Habakkuk's appeal: conviction, a call for action and a cry for mercy.

• A conviction about God's work: 'I stand in awe of your deeds'

Habakkuk's tone has changed from the anxious prayers and appeals of chapter 1. Now he prays with a sense of humble commitment. He is no longer arguing, for he recognizes that everything God has said and done is just. Habakkuk has heard God's Word – the report of God's work in the past as well as the prophecies of what is to come. He has recognized that God is in control and now he accepts God's just purposes. When he prays, 'LORD, I have heard of your fame; I stand in awe of your deeds, LORD', it is a kind of 'amen' to all that God has been saying to him.

- A call for God's action: 'Repeat them in our day'

  Habakkuk longs for God's powerful work in the past to be seen in his own day, so that people would know God is in charge of their lives and history. Chapter 3 has many references to the story of the exodus, celebrated frequently by the psalmists and the prophets as Israel's finest hour. And so Habakkuk appeals, 'Lord, repeat that kind of redemption now.' And he is clear about what matters: renew *your* work. He wants God's purposes fulfilled; God's work established in his day. Essentially, Habakkuk is saying, 'Your kingdom come, your will be done.'

- A cry for God's mercy: 'in wrath remember mercy'

  Habakkuk had heard of God's judgment on his own people in Judah, the fearful reality of God's anger against sin. So he prays that, alongside this, God would remember mercy. Once again, this is a model for us. The essence of prayer is to plead God's character in God's presence (see Numbers 14:10–19). Habakkuk is crying out to God to be true to his character. Wrath and mercy are both essential character traits of God. For example, in Exodus 34:6–7, God is described as 'the compassionate and gracious God . . . Yet he does not leave the guilty unpunished' (see also Romans 11:22). Wrath and mercy are also found together at the heart of the Christian gospel. We know that our rebellion deserves God's anger, so we too cry out for God to be merciful on the grounds of Christ's work on the cross. Habakkuk certainly teaches us about the inevitability of God's wrath, but how wonderful it is that he also points us towards the Lord who shows mercy, the Lord who redeems his people.

Is this the kind of prayer you normally pray? Today, use Habakkuk's prayer as a model for your own.

- Thank God that he is in control of our lives and world.
- Plead with God to renew his church and fulfil his purposes in our generation: 'Your kingdom come; your will be done.'
- Appeal to God: 'in wrath remember mercy'.

Luke and John

Dr Luke, a companion of the apostle Paul, and John, one of Jesus' closest disciples (John 13:23), both wrote accounts of Jesus' life and ministry. John spent three years with Jesus; Luke investigated and recorded the eye-witness testimony he received from others. Both Gospels emphasize the importance of prayer and show Jesus modelling prayer for us.

Luke

Luke wrote for Theophilus, possibly his patron, and for every subsequent believer, 'that you may know the certainty of the things you have been taught' (1:4). His Gospel highlights the place of the Gentiles in God's plan and shows special concern for the poor and for women. Luke summed up Jesus' mission: 'The Son of Man came to seek and to save the lost' (19:10). Through parables, teaching and the example of Jesus, Luke encourages us to be diligent in prayer.

John

The purpose of John's eyewitness testimony of Jesus' life and ministry was: 'that you may believe that Jesus is the Messiah, the Son of God, and that by believing you may have life in his name' (20:31). Chapters 12 – 19 focus exclusively on Jesus' last week – the Last Supper, his final teaching, as well as his trial and crucifixion. Chapter 17 offers a rare insight into Jesus' priorities, as we see him pray for himself, his disciples and all believers.

Day 11

Read: Luke 22:7–34
Key verses: Luke 22:31–32

....

31Simon, Simon, Satan has asked to sift all of you as wheat. 32But I have prayed for you, Simon, that your faith may not fail. And when you have turned back, strengthen your brothers.

Prayer is a key theme in Luke's Gospel. It is Luke who tells us that Jesus was praying when he was baptized and when he was transfigured. Chapter 11 provides teaching about prayer, and chapter 18 recalls parables about prayer, such as that of the persistent widow. The passion narrative in chapters 22 – 23 goes further. Jesus is saying, 'I'm not just teaching you about prayer. I'm doing it, for you.'

This story above, in verses 31–34, was not included in the Gospel account simply to tell the early church that, at a particular moment, Jesus prayed for Simon Peter. Luke's a theologian, so he knows the great truths that the apostle Paul and others communicated regarding the high priestly ministry of Jesus, including the one given in Hebrews 7:25 that Jesus lives for ever to intercede for us. Indeed, it is fascinating that the New Testament letters addressed to persecuted believers extol the high-priestly ministry of Jesus. We find this not only in the letter to the Hebrews, written to Christians in danger of giving up under pressure, but also in Romans 8:34. Similarly, the book of Revelation, written to the seven churches in the province of Asia facing marginalization, prison and even death for their faith, portrays Jesus as a priest. John's vision shows Jesus clothed with a robe reaching to his feet, which was how priests dressed (Revelation 1:13). Luke included this story in his Gospel to remind the early church *that Jesus was praying for them*. In dark times, be encouraged, Jesus is praying for you. Your name has been mentioned in heaven today!

Jesus knew the pressures Peter would go through, so he prayed that his faith would not fail. This prayer was answered. Peter's courage failed but not his faith, unlike Judas, who abandoned his trust in Jesus. Peter was brought to a place of penitence, forgiveness, renewed grace and mercy. As a result, he did 'strengthen his brothers' – many churches all over Asia Minor received, and were blessed by, Peter's first and second letters.

No doubt reflecting on his personal experience of failure and betraying Jesus caused Peter to write, 'Your enemy the devil prowls around like a roaring lion looking for someone to devour' (1 Peter 5:8). You may hear the lion roar as you battle with ill-health, family struggles, temptations, conflict in the church, or mocking at work or at home. But remember that Jesus is praying for you. He is your advocate and, on the basis of his own obedience and righteousness, he is interceding for you. Without the Lord's prayers, we would all end up like Judas – giving up on God and giving in to sin. Today, thank Jesus for his never-ending commitment to you and for his prayers that strengthen and sustain.

Day 12

Read: Luke 22:39 – 23:49
Key verses: Luke 22:42; 23:33–34, 46

....

22:42'Father, if you are willing, take this cup from me; yet not my will, but yours be done' . . . 23:33When they came to the place called the Skull, they crucified him there, along with the criminals – one on his right, the other on his left. 34Jesus said, 'Father, forgive them, for they do not know what they are doing' . . . 46Jesus called out with a loud voice, 'Father, into your hands I commit my spirit.' When he had said this, he breathed his last.

In his last few hours of his life, Jesus cried out to his Father three times, revealing to us his priorities in prayer.

In the Garden of Gethsemane, full of anguish as he thought of bearing the world's sin in his own body, Jesus prayed, 'Father . . . not my will, but yours be done.' He didn't want to please himself; he wanted to please God.

In the same way, what should matter most to us, what should galvanize our praying, is doing the will of God.

The second time Jesus cried out to his Father was in Luke 23:34. When the soldiers drove the nails into his hands, the first thing he said was, 'Father, forgive them, for they do not know what they are doing.' They didn't realize the horror of crucifying the Son of God, the Lord of Glory. Stephen, the first Christian martyr, followed in Jesus' footsteps. As members of the Sanhedrin hurled great stones and accused him of blasphemy, he knelt down and prayed, 'Lord, do not hold this sin against them' (Acts 7:60).

Are you willing to pardon others? To do so must be a priority because our prayers cannot find a hearing in the presence of a holy, loving and just God if we are harbouring bitterness (Matthew 6:15). If you pardon those who have been unkind to you, you will pray for them, which will transform your attitude. Sadly, we find broken relationships where Christians have not prayed for one another. If they had done, the breakdown most likely would not have happened.

The third time Jesus prayed to his Father was in Luke 23:46. The curtain of the temple had been torn in two, and he cried, 'Father, into your hands I commit my spirit.' On the cross, Jesus was quoting Psalm 31:5, expressing his trust in God. In the most bewildering and painful experiences of life, we can say to God, 'Into your hands I commit my spirit.' Jesus was on the threshold of death, facing a journey we will all make unless the Saviour comes first and takes us in triumph to himself. When faced with that journey, we can come to our Father who loves us and we can rest safely in his arms.

Of course, God wants us to ask for things in prayer, but he also wants us to have the right priorities because, if we have the right priorities, we ask for the right things.

Today, as you come to your heavenly Father in prayer, express your

- desire to do his will;
- love for his people;
- trust in his sovereignty.

Day 13

Read: John 17:1–26
Key verses: John 17:1–4

....

¹*Father, the hour has come. Glorify your Son, that your Son may glorify you.* ²*For you granted him authority over all people that he might give eternal life to all those you have given him.* ³*Now this is eternal life: that they know you, the only true God, and Jesus Christ, whom you have sent.* ⁴*I have brought you glory on earth by finishing the work you gave me to do.*

We are standing on holy ground. We are reading the words said by one member of the Trinity to another – Jesus' praying to his Father. He knows that the 'hour' – the time for the cross – has come. Out of the depths of his sorrow Jesus expresses his ultimate longing for this act of self-sacrifice to glorify his Father (John 12:27–28).

How does Jesus glorify the Father?

• By the giving of eternal life (verses 2–3)

Human responsibility to respond to the gospel message is not denied, but these verses portray salvation, from the perspective of the Father and the Son, as God's sovereign gift of grace to us. The substance of eternal life is knowing God; that's what the Christian life is all about and that brings glory to the Father.

How can we glorify God? God is supremely glorified by the mission of his Son (sent into the world by the Father), which becomes the mission of the church (sent into the world by the Son). For the Lord's glory, for his honour, we are motivated to share the good news that people might enter into eternal life.

• By the completion of the work (verse 4)

Individually, *we* are not called to win the world for Christ. The *church* is called to win the world for Christ. We are called to find out, within that total purpose of God, what our roles are and to fulfil them with all our might – this glorifies God. Remember, Jesus too had limitations set on him during his life: he didn't ever leave the Holy Land; his teaching and healing didn't reach more than a few thousand at any one time; he didn't ever know the intimacies of marriage, the struggles of parenthood, the challenges of middle age or the limitations of ageing. Yet he brought glory to the Father because he did what he was called to do perfectly and completely, with single-minded dedication and, at the end, he could say, 'I have glorified your name.'

When we can begin to pray 'Father, glorify your name' meaningfully, making it a fundamental motivation of our lives, we are maturing as Christians and becoming more like the Lord Jesus.

Heavenly Father, help me to glorify your name by sharing the gospel and living it out where you have placed me. Help me to be obedient to you today when I'm at work, looking after family, relaxing with friends and serving in church. May I be single-minded in my dedication to you, like King David who 'served God's purpose in his own generation' (Acts 13:36).

Day 14

Read: John 17:1–26
Key verses: John 17:11, 14–15

••

> [11]*I will remain in the world no longer, but they are still in the world, and I am coming to you. Holy Father, protect them by the power of your name, the name you gave me, so that they may be one as we are one . . .* [14]*I have given them your word and the world has hated them, for they are not of the world any more than I am of the world.* [15]*My prayer is not that you take them out of the world but that you protect them from the evil one.*

What does Jesus pray for his friends?

Jesus prayed for protection from the world which hated them (verse 14). He spelled this out in more detail earlier (15:18–25). It is not that we go out of our way to make the world hate us. On the contrary, we love the world, we get involved in the world, we care for people and we are as winsome as we possibly can be in our witness. We don't set out to be hated but, inevitably, we are; we follow a different leader and our value system is necessarily different because of our loyalty to Christ.

We also need protection from the evil one (verse 15); we need to be alert to the real opposition of the devil. Jesus prays that the power of the name of God would protect the disciples. The name of God is the revealed character of God; our protection comes from committing ourselves to him and reminding ourselves of who he is. 'The name of the LORD is a strong tower. The righteous run in to it and are safe' (Proverbs 18:10, NKJV). Protection is in the name of the Lord, in the character of God and in who God is. Throughout his ministry, Jesus revealed the Father and did so in this prayer, which teaches us about the Father's love, his ownership of his people and his sovereign purpose. It is in these things, as we lay hold of them and affirm them, that we find our protection.

Notice that this protection is corporate. Verse 11 continues, 'so that they may be one as we are one'. We often forget that all the basic New Testament teaching is given in letters to churches and is meant to be understood corporately. The Christian life is not envisaged in terms of individuals living in isolation, but in terms of commitment to a community in which each one is loved, prayed for, supported and encouraged. It is in community that we find strength and protection too.

Jesus is praying for your protection, which is found in God alone. Today, turn to your heavenly Father for refuge, security and strength.

Whoever dwells in the shelter of the Most High
will rest in the shadow of the Almighty.
I will say of the LORD, 'He is my refuge and my
fortress,
my God, in whom I trust' . . .

He will cover you with his feathers,
and under his wings you will find refuge;
his faithfulness will be your shield and rampart.
(Psalm 91:1–2, 4)

Day 15

Read: John 17:1–26
Key verses: John 17:13, 17–19

....

> [13] *I am coming to you now, but I say these things while I am still in the world, so that they may have the full measure of my joy within them . . .* [17] *Sanctify them by the truth; your word is truth.* [18] *As you sent me into the world, I have sent them into the world.* [19] *For them I sanctify myself, that they too may be truly sanctified.*

Amid all the grim, costly conflict of the Christian disciple's life, Jesus makes an astounding prayer request: he prays that you'll be delighted (verse 13). Our Lord wants his disciples to have 'the full measure of my joy within them'. He wants us to have the joy of the kingdom, Christ and his resurrection; the joy of his presence, heaven and the victories of his grace; the joy that he had, in spite of his suffering, when he went to the cross.

Perhaps less surprising is his final prayer for his disciples. He prays that they may be dedicated to God's mission in the world. Being set apart for mission is enabled on two fronts: through the truth – by living in and under the truth of God, illumined by the Spirit of God (verse 17); and by Jesus, who lays himself on the altar: 'For them I sanctify myself' (verse 19). It's in his sanctification that we find the resources for our being set apart for the sake of the world. This is a very holy moment. Here is the Son, coming again to the Father, in self-giving. Although our Lord came out of eternity in the purpose of God to give himself (which he affirmed again and again through his mission), he arrived at the cross and, once again, there was a need for another moment of commitment. We sometimes talk about giving our lives to God, but we can't give our lives in one moment. All we can give is that moment. It takes a lifetime to give a lifetime to God.

Jesus prays for us to have joy in our discipleship. He's not praying for us to have a moment of elation or a 'glass half-full' attitude; he is praying for us to love and obey him, the source of true joy:

> As the Father has loved me, so have I loved you. Now remain in my love. If you keep my commands, you will remain in my love, just as I have kept my Father's

commands and remain in his love. I have told you this so that my joy may be in you and that your joy may be complete.

(John 15:9–11)

Such love and obedience inevitably lead to our fulfilling God's mission in the world as we live in and under the truth of Scripture and rely on Jesus' resources. Like Jesus, our lifetime of surrender to God is given moment by moment. Today, meditate on Jesus' prayer for you and give this moment to God.

Day 16

Read: John 17:1–26
Key verses: John 17:20–23

....

[20]My prayer is not for them alone. I pray also for those who will believe in me through their message, [21]that all of them may be one, Father, just as you are in me and I am in you. May they also be in us so that the world may believe that you have sent me. [22]I have given them the glory that you gave me, that they may be one as we are one – [23]I in them and you in me – so that they may be brought to complete unity. Then the world will know that you sent me and have loved them even as you have loved me.

Jesus prayed for us! He didn't just pray for his disciples but for all those who would believe through their message. He prayed for us to be united. This unity is supernatural, tangible and evangelical.

- Supernatural

  It is given by the Spirit. We are born again and therefore share this common life of God.

- Tangible

  The world has to see it to believe it.

- Evangelical

  It is not simply a unity of love; it is unity predicated on adherence to the revelation of the Father through the Son. There are moments, despite our commitment to this unity, when we might have to say 'no' if we believe that the revelation of God through Jesus is in question.

In our local churches, when people come to an enquirers' course, they need to encounter a unity that reflects the reality of Christ and his love. With all the divisions in our culture, we have a marvellous evangelistic opportunity to embody the values of the kingdom in our communities. Jesus finishes by praying that his mission would be completed by our sharing and seeing his glory (verses 24–26).

Read through John 17:1–26 again. Why does the Holy Spirit give us this prayer at this point in the biblical record? Look back to John 16:23–24: 'Very truly I tell you, my Father will give you whatever you ask in my name . . . Ask and you will receive.' Jesus is saying that prayer in Jesus' name is guaranteed an answer. The answer might be 'no', but God will always answer prayer in Jesus' name. If he's committed to do that, how much more will God answer Jesus' prayer in Jesus' name? Jesus, on the brink of his self-sacrifice, is gathering up in his arms all the generations of the people of God, all our witness, mission, ministry, service and faith, and he presents them before the Father. God the Father says 'amen' to it; the prayer of Jesus is irresistible. Despite calamities, terror and martyrdom, we will be protected, united, delighted, dedicated, completed and glorified because Jesus prayed for us.

As you meditate on the scope of Jesus' prayer for you in John 17, make this prayer your own:

Lord Jesus, because you ever live to pray for us, may we ever more quickly abandon ourselves to you and your advocacy. Certainly, anything and everything you pray for will come to pass. Your advocacy is our assurance; your intercession is our liberation; your prayers are our peace. Thank you, and hallelujah!

(Scotty Smith, *Every Season Prayers*, Baker, 2016, p. 66)

Ephesians, Philippians and 1 Thessalonians

The apostle Paul was a prolific letter writer. He wrote to churches and individuals on a variety of subjects and, in each letter, he included his prayer for the believers to whom he was writing. For us, each prayer is a treasure trove of core spiritual truths and steers us towards the priorities we should have as we pray for ourselves and for others.

Ephesians

'God's high calling for the church' is the resounding theme of Ephesians. Paul had stayed in Ephesus for three years, planting a church. This commercial centre was a strategic place for evangelism, from which the gospel spread to the surrounding communities. No doubt Paul's letter was intended to be circulated to all the churches in the area. He writes that the church displays God's 'manifold wisdom' (Ephesians 3:10) and prays that, as these believers come to understand their spiritual blessings and eternal inheritance, they would rely on Jesus' resurrection power and come to know God better.

Philippians

Paul is writing to the church in the Roman colony of Philippi to thank them for their financial gift and update them on his work. He writes about a wide range of areas related to Christian living. He exhorts them to 'rejoice in the Lord' (4:4), live in humility and unity, and stand firm in the face of persecution. He warns them against legalists and libertines. He prays for the love they have for one another to continue to grow.

1 Thessalonians

The first epistle to the Thessalonians is essentially a follow-up letter to new Christians. Persecution forced Paul and his companions to flee the busy seaport city of Thessalonica sooner than he would have wished, leaving behind a group of very new Jewish and Gentile converts (Acts 17:1–10). Paul wrote to these believers from Corinth to encourage them to stand firm in persecution. The letter also provides instruction about the second coming of Christ that he had hoped to give in person. He prays for these believers, who had started off so well, to continue to make spiritual progress.

Day 17

Read: Ephesians 1:1–23
Key verses: Ephesians 1:15–16

••

> *15For this reason, ever since I heard about your faith in the Lord Jesus and your love for all God's people, 16I have not stopped giving thanks for you, remembering you in my prayers.*

I reckon I use about 3% of the capacity of my mobile phone. I'm only scratching the surface of everything it could do for me. The same seems to be true when it comes to our spiritual blessings – we don't fully grasp what we've been given and the difference it could make. Ephesians 1 tells me I'm chosen, God is sovereign, I'm adopted as a son, God has filled me with his Spirit and I have a tremendous future ahead. We're spiritual millionaires and yet we live like paupers, pathetically unaware of how rich we really are.

Paul is thrilled as he prays, remembering these spiritual blessings and all that God has been doing behind the scenes of history for the Ephesian congregation. The church exists because God has been at work 'before the creation of the world' (verse 4). In terms of putting together a body of believers, Isaiah says that God carved my name and those of my brothers and sisters in his hand before the beginning of time (Isaiah 49:16). Talk about the value that God places on us!

Jesus' death brings us 'redemption through his blood, the forgiveness of sins, in accordance with the riches of God's grace' (verse 7). This means that, amazingly, believers are a family, despite the immense barriers of race, class, culture, intellect and age. Paul goes on, 'And you also were included in Christ' and his Spirit made you a new creation, having believed, 'you were marked in him with a seal, the promised Holy Spirit' (verse 13). So God carved my name in his hand and he sent the Lord Jesus to die. Then he sent the Holy Spirit to turn my heart around when I was fully against him, which is no small thing. One day, I'll stand before God and he'll say, 'Rico, it's good to see you. You've been on my mind a very long time.'

If Paul came to your church on a Sunday morning, he'd grab your arm and he'd say, 'Look at these people. This is the evidence that God's mighty plan for the redemption of the world is working out, and you're part of it! It's amazing!'

This prompts me to ask, do you love and marvel at your local church?

How often do you pray for your church? You may occasionally pray for church ministries or leaders, but most of us don't often pray that we would grasp our spiritual blessings fully!

Today, take time to meditate on Ephesians 1:3–14 and thank God for your church and all the spiritual blessings you enjoy. Allow these truths to seep deeply into your soul and affect not only your prayer life but also your actions and attitudes.

Day 18

Read: Ephesians 1:1–23
Key verse: Ephesians 1:17

···

I keep asking that the God of our Lord Jesus Christ, the glorious Father, may give you the Spirit of wisdom and revelation, so that you may know him better.

In the midst of suffering, struggles and the challenges of everyday life, what are you praying for? Paul prays for spiritual enlightenment. He prays for the Ephesians to know God better. The original words translated 'knowledge' in our Bibles can have a much richer range of use than our word 'knowledge'. The King James Version helps us see this in the Old Testament because it says, 'Adam knew Eve . . . and she conceived'; 'Cain knew his wife and she conceived' (Genesis 4:1, 17). The Bible uses this word *yada* ('know') for sex. The Greek word here, like that Hebrew word, often speaks not of information but of personal encounter. Paul prays here that you may *know*

God in the depths, that you may personally, intimately encounter him. Isn't that staggering?

Doubtless, along with persecution, the Ephesians faced economic, social and relational problems, and yet Paul does not pray for easier circumstances – rest for the stressed, health for the sick, success for the struggling. He doesn't pray for their circumstances at all. If that were me, I'd pray, 'Give me rest, health and success, because I feel stressed, sick and struggling!' When we pray for ourselves and others, we need to be praying more like Paul, 'Lord, you know that John is really struggling with his illness. You know how worried I am about the pressures of Claire's new job, and how stressed Paul and Fiona are about selling their flat. But thank you that they are Christian believers and you've blessed them in Christ with every spiritual blessing. Please open their eyes to grasp what you've done for them and help them know you better.' It may seem tame to pray for the grasping of invisible truths and the changing of inward character – what about the illness, the stress and the sale of the flat? But Paul knows that if people know God, then whatever issues arise stay in perspective.

The point is not that we never pray about our jobs, house moves or family issues, but that through all the circumstances of our lives – good and bad – our priority, our prayer, is that we may know God better. As Paul said in Philippians 3:8–11:

> I consider everything a loss because of the surpassing worth of knowing Christ Jesus my Lord, for whose sake I have lost all things. I consider them garbage, that I may gain Christ and be found in him, not having a righteousness of my own that comes from the law, but that which is through faith in Christ – the righteousness that comes from God on the basis of faith. I want to know Christ – yes, to know the power of his resurrection and participation in his sufferings, becoming like him in his death, and so, somehow, attaining to the resurrection from the dead.

Day 19

Read: Ephesians 1:1–23
Key verse: Ephesians 1:18

....

I pray that the eyes of your heart may be enlightened in order that you may know the hope to which he has called you, the riches of his glorious inheritance in his holy people.

I always wanted more. I never had enough milk or money or socks or sex or holidays or first editions or solitude or gramophone records or free meals or real friends or guilt-less pleasure or neckties or applause or unquestioning love. Of course, I've had more than my share of most of these commodities, but it always left me with a vague feeling of unfulfilment.

These are the opening words of the autobiography of Barry Humphries (Dame Edna Everage), entitled *More Please* (Penguin, 2016).

The human heart is always asking for 'more, please'. We have an insatiable desire for beauty, peace, rest, happiness and love. We seek to satisfy these desires within the parameters of this world, but whatever we do never quite measures up, never quite quenches our thirst. The problem is we are looking to the world to satisfy eternal desires. The Bible teaches us that God has set eternity in our hearts (Ecclesiastes 3:11), and that desire for eternity will only be satisfied with the treasures of eternity. So, God means for that desire for beauty, rest, peace, love and happiness to be satisfied not just in him here on earth but in the full knowledge of God in the world to come. And it will *not* be satisfied anywhere else.

Paul particularly prays 'that the eyes of your heart may be [opened to] the hope to which he has called you' because, if we don't grasp what a great eternity each of us has ahead of us, our temptation will always be to build heaven here. Ephesians 1 reminds us that we are going to inherit the earth and, in Christ, the future is ours, so we shouldn't try to build heaven now. Instead, it is best to invest our time and energy in God's purposes.

If my aim is to build heaven here, then it becomes hard to submit to Christ, love him and share him with others. I don't speak about Christ because I don't want to cause any upset; I don't want to be drawn into other people's problems; I want heaven here. Financial giving? I can't do that because I'm building heaven here. God's going to have to be happy with the small change. Regular prayer and personal Bible reading are going to be a struggle because I've got heaven here to worry about. Involvement with small groups and discipleship courses is not an option. I'm casual about church membership because my focus is building heaven here.

What are your treasures? Where are you building?

Are you trying to build heaven on earth? Examine your relationships, bank statement and diary to find out in whom and what you are investing your life. Today, pray that you will fully grasp the hope and inheritance you have, and that these eternal realities will shape your life now.

If you read history, you will find that the Christians who did most for the present world were just those who thought most of the next.

(C. S. Lewis, *Mere Christianity*, Collins, 2016, p. 132)

Day 20

Read: Ephesians 1:1–23
Key verses: Ephesians 1:18–20

....

> [18] *I pray that the eyes of your heart may be enlightened in order that you may know* . . . [19] *his incomparably great power for us who believe. That power is the same as the mighty strength* [20] *he exerted when he raised Christ from the dead and seated him at his right hand in the heavenly realms.*

Do you feel trapped in a cycle of sin, a pattern of behaviour you just can't seem to escape from? Is there a secret sin you have been indulging in? Have you grown accustomed to excusing the so-called 'respectable sins', such as gossip, worry, gluttony and lack of contentment? There is hope; you can change. Here, Paul prays that these Ephesian believers – and we – might know that we are possessed by God's power. Paul wants us to see that not only do we have a glorious inheritance, a wonderful future, but we also have God's power at work in us now.

You are sitting on a gold mine! The power that raised Christ, seated him at God's right hand and placed him above every power and authority we might tremble at is already at work in us. This means that we can pray, 'Lord, I'm angry at this person, but thank you that the power that raised Christ from the dead is at work in me. Please help me to calm down and be godly. Please, Lord, give me your Spirit and your strength to comfort and calm me.' Don't look inwards at yourself or sideways at one another; look to Christ and know that you are possessed by the same power.

When you are feeling weak, insecure and struggling with sin, ask him for strength to control your tongue, temper, lust, greed, malice and jealousy. If you look to Christ and fill your heart with him, you can battle against your sinful nature as you need to each day. Do you think it is beyond the power of God, who raised Christ from the dead, to help you? It is beyond our power, yes, but it is certainly not beyond God's power.

Today, as you wrestle with the temptation to sin, will you remember that the same power that raised Jesus from the dead is available to you? Pray for God's 'mighty strength' to help you 'to say "No" to ungodliness and worldly passions, and to live self-controlled, upright and godly lives in this present age' (Titus 2:12).

> A cry for help from the heart of a childlike [believer] is sweet praise in the ears of God. Nothing exalts Him more than the collapse of self-reliance which issues in passionate prayer for help. 'Call upon me in the day of trouble; I will deliver you, and you shall glorify me' (Ps. 50:15). Prayer is the translation into a thousand different words of a single sentence: 'Apart from me [Christ], you can do nothing' (John 15:5).
> (John Piper, *Brothers, We Are Not Professionals*, Broadman & Holman, 2013, p. 70)

Day 21

Read: Ephesians 6:10–20
Key verses: Ephesians 6:18–20

....

> [18]*And pray in the Spirit on all occasions with all kinds of prayers and requests. With this in mind, be alert and always keep on praying for all the Lord's people.* [19]*Pray also for me, that whenever I speak, words may be given me so that I will fearlessly make known the mystery of the gospel,* [20]*for which I am an ambassador in chains. Pray that I may declare it fearlessly, as I should.*

Just as the armour of God is not reserved for the spiritual elite, neither is praying. Prayer is indispensable if we are to stand strong and resolute in our faith (Ephesians 6:10, 11, 13, 14).

Paul urges us to 'pray in the Spirit', that is, to pray prayers which are energized by the Spirit of God. Pray with thanksgiving, petitions and intercessions; pray silently, vocally, individually and corporately; fast from food, hold all-night prayer vigils – all these are included when Paul says pray 'with all kinds of prayers and requests' (verse 18).

In verse 19, he adds, 'Pray also for me.' Although Paul had written almost half the New Testament and preached throughout the then-known world, he is asking for prayer. Although he has raised a man from the dead (Acts 20:10) and cast out demons (Acts 16:18), he is asking for prayer. Although he has gone up to the third heaven and heard things that human beings are not allowed to hear (2 Corinthians 12:2–4), he is asking for prayer. Paul recognized his need for prayer. He acknowledged his utter dependence on God's power and enabling for his life and ministry. In contrast, we often become too *self*-focused in our ministries. We try to deal with problems in our own strength, to the extent that we almost stigmatize praying. We behave as if we believe that to need prayer is to need a crutch.

What did Paul want the believers to pray for? First, for his preaching to be energized by God as God's Word was proclaimed. Second, for fearless proclamation, that he would not be shy as he shared the 'mystery of the gospel'. Third, that he would be an ambassador for Christ, even in his prison cell. We need to pray for the things that burn in God's heart – concern for those who have not heard the gospel, the preaching of the Word – to burn in our hearts too.

We may pray for our church leaders occasionally but often only in a general sense. Today, will you pray specifically for the person who is preparing to preach in your church this Sunday? Pray for the

- preaching to be energized by God;
- proclamation of the gospel to be fearless, regardless of potential opposition;
- life to authenticate the message.

Pray too for your church congregation who will listen to the message this Sunday. Pray for unbelievers to accept the gospel joyfully and for believers to respond in obedience. Don't forget to pray for yourself – for the things that burn in God's heart to burn ever more strongly and brightly in yours.

Day 22

Read: Philippians 1:1–11
Key verse: Philippians 1:9

....

*And this is my prayer: that your love may abound
more and more in knowledge and depth of insight.*

What is the biggest problem in the church? People!
We struggle to get on with one another. Philippi was the
definition of a loving church and yet, even here, there are
problems. In chapter 2, Paul has to say to the believers,
'Look, you need to have the mind of Christ, who humbled
himself so much and was obedient to death.' In Philippians
4:2, we are told that there are two women who can't
agree. Consequently, Paul's main prayer for this church
is love. He prays for an *abounding* love. Paul wants the
believers to demonstrate a love for one another that is
growing, increasing, bubbling up and overflowing.

My family and I used to live near Malvern and, as far as I
am aware, the Malvern spring has never run dry. Even in
the driest periods, the water continues to bubble up and

flow out. That's the kind of love that Paul is talking about here. Are there people in your fellowship with whom you don't get on? Are there people you don't speak to or have a certain level of bitterness towards? Well, you need to pray for the Lord to give you the kind of love that bubbles up and flows out.

What about our lost world? On a hot day, I would love to be in Malvern, standing under the Malvern spring, its cold, refreshing water flowing over me. Wouldn't you? In this world, where there is so much pain and sorrow, the church is supposed to be a spring of overflowing love. Yes, we must preach the truth in Christ. Even so, what makes people sit up and take notice of Christianity is seeing Christians who love one another – that's where it starts. Sooner or later, they can hear the gospel, but the thing that will attract them first and foremost is the life-refreshing spring of love that flows up and flows out.

Notice here that Paul is not only praying for an abounding love but also an *intelligent* love. In verse 9, Paul prays for a love abounding 'in knowledge and depth of insight'. Christian love is not mere sentiment; it knows the truth, and is rooted in knowledge and understanding.

Do you dare pray for more love? More love will result in more prayer! Watch out for this delightful pattern emerging in your life.

> Prayer is the product of [our] passion for people ... Unaffected fervency in prayer is not whipped-up emotionalism, but the overflow of [our] love for brothers and sisters in Christ Jesus. That means that if we are to improve our praying, we must strengthen our loving. As we grow in disciplined, self-sacrificing love, so we will grow in intercessory prayer. Superficially fervent prayers devoid of such love are finally phony, hollow, shallow.
> (D. A. Carson, *A Call to Spiritual Reformation*, IVP, 2011, p. 85)

Day 23

Read: Philippians 1:1–11
Key verses: Philippians 1:9–11

....

> [9]And this is my prayer: that your love may abound more and more in knowledge and depth of insight, [10]so that you may be able to discern what is best and may be pure and blameless for the day of Christ, [11]filled with the fruit of righteousness that comes through Jesus Christ – to the glory and praise of God.

Why should we pray for love? Because, if we love one another with God's overflowing love, three things will follow: discernment, purity and the fruit of righteousness.

• Discernment

Verse 10 says, 'so that you may be able to discern what is *best*' (my emphasis). If you have love from God for one another, you will be able to make a judgment about what is important and what isn't, the things that really matter and the things that don't.

Some years ago, I was President of the Fellowship of Independent Evangelical Churches (FIEC). There are almost 600 churches in FIEC and I travelled all over the country helping those in trouble. I still visit churches and I have yet to find one in which the things that divide Christians are actually fundamental, biblical or theological principles. Almost always, the division is over secondary things, issues of culture or preference, such as sung worship.

What are the things that are troubling your church at the moment? Are they *really* theological things? The Bible says that love covers a multitude of sins, a multitude of differences, and that love will give you discernment.

• Purity

Verse 10 also says, '[so that you] may be pure and blameless for the day of Christ'. The word 'pure' means 'chaste'; the word 'blameless' conveys the idea of not causing other people to stumble. Paul prays for these believers to be abounding in love, because if you love your brothers and sisters in the church, you will make sure you do nothing to cause them to stumble. Why? Because you know that you are going to heaven together. You know that you belong to one another. You know that Christ is coming and, when he does come, every sin will be revealed in the blaze of his glory!

- The fruit of righteousness

Overflowing love leads to being 'filled with the fruit of righteousness' (verse 11). Essentially, 'the fruit of righteousness' means being filled with love, grace and mercy towards one another. It means being filled with the fruit of the Spirit. And, as Galatians 5 emphasizes, the fruit of the Spirit is displayed within the context of relationships.

God wants to enlarge our hearts and increase our capacity for loving him and others.

Father, please pour out the Spirit upon us in increased measure. Save us from paddling around in the shallows of limited vision and understanding, and please sweep us up in the ocean of your matchless love. Lord, forgive my small view of your vast generosity, and grant that every thought of your Fatherly care may cause my love for your Son Jesus to deepen and then overflow, so that others may be caught up in your embrace. For the sake of Jesus, in whose name I pray, Amen.

(Alistair Begg, *Pray Big*, Good Book Company, 2019, pp. 83–84)

Day 24

Read: Philippians 1:1–11
Key verses: Philippians 1:9–11

....

⁹And this is my prayer: that your love may abound more and more in knowledge and depth of insight, ¹⁰so that you may be able to discern what is best and may be pure and blameless for the day of Christ, ¹¹filled with the fruit of righteousness that comes through Jesus Christ – to the glory and praise of God.

Why should we pray this prayer of the Bible for ourselves and make it our own? So that we may be 'to the glory and praise of God'. God's great concern is for his glory. All of creation, every starry constellation, displays God's glory. The psalmist declared, 'The heavens declare the glory of God' (Psalm 19:1). Supremely, God's glory is seen in the face of his Son, Jesus Christ (2 Corinthians 4:6). But, amazingly, God's glory is also seen in his people, the church, as Ephesians 3:20–21 highlights:

> Now to him to is able to do immeasurably more than all we ask or imagine, according to his power that is at work within us, to him be glory in the church and in Christ Jesus throughout all generations, for ever and ever! Amen.

Can you believe it – 'glory in the church'? Glory in your church, with all its foibles, failings and imperfections. Paul thought of this church in Philippi that had stood by him through thick and thin, and he prayed for its people to love one another. As they loved one another as he loved them, as they loved him, as they moved in the love of God, he prayed for the world to see it and for God to be glorified. This is the work of the church – to show people the glory of God.

On the walls of the Faith Mission building in Edinburgh there's a quote from the US evangelist, D. L. Moody: 'Out of 100 men, one will read the Bible, the other 99 will read the Christian.' What will the world see? Where will they see the gospel? They'll see it in you. Our job as individuals in the church is to make Jesus Christ visible, intelligible and desirable. That is the essence of Paul's prayer.

> Praying over the Word . . . has the effect of shaping our minds and hearts, so that we desire what the Word encourages us to desire, and not just what we desire by nature. That is why the prayers of Bible-saturated people

sound so differently. Most people, before their prayers are soaked in Scripture, simply bring their natural desires to God. In other words, they pray the way an unbeliever would pray who is convinced that God might give him what he wants: health, a better job, safe journeys, a prosperous portfolio, successful children, plenty of food, a happy marriage, a car that works, a comfortable retirement, etc. None of these is evil. They're just natural. You don't have to be born again to want any of these. Desiring them – even from God – is no evidence of saving faith. So if these are all you pray for, there is a deep problem. Your desires have not yet been changed to put the glory of Christ at the center.

(John Piper, *When I Don't Desire God*, Crossway, 2013, p. 165)

Day 25

Read: 1 Thessalonians 3:6–13
Key verse: 1 Thessalonians 3:10

•••

Night and day we pray most earnestly that we may see you again and supply what is lacking in your faith.

Are you growing?

Paul tells these Thessalonian Christians that he's heard about their faith, love and hope (1 Thessalonians 1:3). His prayer is that these wonderful virtues may keep on growing (1 Thessalonians 5:8). If you're not growing as a Christian, then there's something wrong. You don't stand still in the Christian life. You either go forwards or backwards, but you never, ever, stand still.

The first aspect of Paul's prayer is that the Thessalonians' faith may be strengthened (verse 10). Persecution had forced Paul to leave Thessalonica in a hurry, and he longs to see the believers again. He's been praying for them, he's written to them, he's sent Timothy to them, but he longs to see them. Why? He wants to strengthen their faith. Paul is not talking about the experience of faith, more about Christian truth. There's something lacking in their understanding of Christian truth that he wants to teach them. One clear gap in their theology was the issue of what happened to people who died before the Lord's return (1 Thessalonians 4:13–17).

Paul prays for the Thessalonians' faith and their grasp of truth to grow. He wants them to have a better understanding of God's Word so that they can increase their knowledge of the Lord Jesus. The Bible is about Jesus, from beginning to end. The more we know of Jesus, the deeper our love for him becomes and the stronger we are in our Christian lives. Doctrine, the truth of God's Word, is not just for the academics who go to Bible college; it is the warp and weft of our lives. Doctrine is the truth that keeps us going in difficult times. It strengthens us and is the rock-solid foundation of our lives. Paul prays for these Thessalonians because he wants to fill up those bits that are missing in their faith. He wants them to be firmly established so that they will stand strong when trials come (1 Thessalonians 1:6; 2:14–15; 3:2–3).

Is your faith growing? Is your understanding of the Bible growing?

We may pray for health, for God's strength to deal with the challenges of the day, but rarely do we pray to grow in our knowledge and understanding of Christian doctrine. Will you pray that prayer today? What practical measures can you put in place to be the answer to that prayer and grow in your understanding of the Bible? Think about how you listen to sermons, prepare for Bible studies and approach your devotional times with God. Also, reflect on the opportunities you have to teach doctrine – reading Bible stories to your children before bed, singing Christian songs with your grandchildren in the car, leading a Bible study, speaking words of encouragement to another believer. Pray for God to use these moments to increase the faith of others.

Day 26

Read: 1 Thessalonians 3:6–13
Key verse: 1 Thessalonians 3:12

....

May the Lord make your love increase and overflow for each other and for everyone else, just as ours does for you.

Timothy had reported to Paul that the church in Thessalonica was a loving one (1 Thessalonians 1:3). But Paul is not content with the status quo. He prays for the believers, asking for their love for one another to overflow and for their love to overflow to a lost world.

• Their love for one another to overflow

Paul prays for the believers' love for each other to grow, to become stronger and deeper. His great prayer in the New Testament is that the church may demonstrate love between Christians to a lost world (see Philippians 1:9–11, Days 22 and 23). There are twenty-one letters in the New Testament and every single one, at some point, talks about the problem of relationships between Christians. Why? Because loving one another is important, which, because we're all different, is difficult. Do you love one another enough? Of course, our love for one another depends on our love for Christ. We cannot serve the Lord, the Lord's people and a lost world unless our hearts are right in our relationship with Christ.

In Revelation 2:1–7, John writes to the church at Ephesus. It is a busy, doctrinally sound church that has persevered despite persecution. It seems to be a great church, until you read verse 4: 'Yet I hold this against you: you have forsaken the love you had at first.' Literally, the Ephesians have deserted their first love. It is the same word that is used of Peter when he denied the Lord three times. They have denied their first love. Do you love Jesus as much as you used to? If you don't, ask him to give you that love. Only then will you be able to love others.

• Their love to overflow to a lost world

Imagine a spring from which the water never runs dry and to which people flock to quench their thirst. The church is supposed to be like that spring, flowing out of the life of Christ, pointing people to Jesus. Jesus said, 'Whoever believes in me will never be thirsty' (John 6:35). In this world, we're surrounded by lost men and women who are desperate, who go down into the gutter to drink the water. We have the gospel of Jesus Christ; the most loving thing we can do is to tell them this good news and show them it in action. This should be the focus of our prayers and our energies.

Are you willing to say to God that He can have whatever He wants? Do you believe that wholehearted commitment to Him is more important than any other thing or person in your life? Do you know that nothing you do in this life will ever matter, unless it is about loving God and loving the people He has made?

(Francis Chan, *Crazy Love*, David C. Cook Publishing, 2013, p. 97)

Day 27

Read: 1 Thessalonians 3:6–13
Key verse: 1 Thessalonians 3:13

....

May he strengthen your hearts so that you will be blameless and holy in the presence of our God and Father when our Lord Jesus comes with all his holy ones.

The motivation behind Paul's prayer is for the Thessalonian believers to be established and to grow in purity and holiness, ready for Christ's return.

We don't often hear sermons about holiness, despite the Bible's teaching that the purpose of God in salvation is holiness. Before the foundation of the world, the Father chose us in Christ to be holy (Ephesians 1:4). The Son died on the cross, shedding his blood to bring into existence the holy people of God (Colossians 1:12–14; Hebrews 13:12). The Holy Spirit – the secret is in the name – had the agenda to transform us, to make us holy. But what is holiness? It is quite simply the beauty of Christ shining through us. Holiness is being like Jesus. It is a passion for God and his purity, and it is seen in the lives of those who follow Christ.

Paul prays for the Thessalonians to become more and more pure, holy and blameless, because Jesus is coming back. The return of Christ is the heartbeat of 1 Thessalonians. Every chapter in the book begins or ends with this doctrine. If we don't speak about holiness very much, we speak even less about the Lord's return. Perhaps we're a bit confused about the details, but there is one great truth to cling to: Jesus is coming back. As he went, so he will return and when he comes, it will be glorious. He'll bring the angels of heaven and his people with him. The dead in Christ will rise and we will see the Lord for ever.

It is this great and glorious hope that directs our prayers and drives the church on. If we are to be the kind of Christians God wants us to be, we must look forward to the second coming of Christ. We must be like those Thessalonians who 'turned to God from idols to serve the living and true God, and to wait for his Son from heaven . . . Jesus' (1 Thessalonians 1:9–10).

You ought to live holy and godly lives as you look forward to the day of God and speed its coming.
(2 Peter 3:11–12)

For the grace of God has appeared that offers salvation to all people. It teaches us to say 'No' to ungodliness and worldly passions, and to live self-controlled, upright and godly lives in this present age, while we wait for the blessed hope – the appearing of the glory of our great God and Saviour, Jesus Christ.
(Titus 2:11–13)

Today, pray that you would grow in holiness, ready for Christ's return. Ask for God's help to root out sin and to display, in increasing measure, the fruit of the Holy Spirit.

James

Stephen's martyrdom in Jerusalem signalled a mass exodus; believers fled and were scattered throughout the Roman Empire. As the leader of the Jerusalem church, what words of encouragement would James write to these persecuted Christians? Perhaps a little surprisingly, his key message was that faith works. Genuine belief inevitably transforms our speech, suffering, priorities and every other aspect of life. In his characteristic down-to-earth style, James urges believers to pray for wisdom, healing and forgiveness. In just five chapters, he briefly touches upon a variety of issues, urging these followers of Christ to put their faith to work.

Day 28

Read: James 1:1–18
Key verses: James 1:5–8

....

5If any of you lacks wisdom, you should ask God, who gives generously to all without finding fault, and it will be given to you. 6But when you ask, you must believe and not doubt, because the one who doubts is like a wave of the sea, blown and tossed by the wind. 7That person should not expect to receive anything from the Lord. 8Such a person is double-minded and unstable in all they do.

Have you prayed for wisdom lately? Wisdom is discerning the right thing to do; it is seeing as God intends you to see. It is a gift from God and, like Solomon, we have to ask for it (1 Kings 3:9; 4:29). In Ephesians 1 and Colossians 1, we are encouraged to pray for fellow Christians, for them to have wisdom. When we ask, God promises to be so generous in doling out this wisdom that we will be stunned. We will receive so much more than we could ever 'ask or imagine' (Ephesians 3:20).

The problem is, however, that many people pray for wisdom – and other things – while hedging their bets. They don't really believe God is going to answer, but they pray anyway. Prayer is a safety net in case their other options fail. Remember John Bunyan's character in *Pilgrim's Progress*, Mr Facing-Both-Ways? The message of the Sermon on the Mount presses the point home: 'You can't serve God and money . . . You can't store up treasure on heaven and on earth . . . You can't be double-minded.' James explains that if you are double-minded, you have no anchor for your soul. You are like a boat tossed about on a rough sea. The only other place this word is used is in Luke 8, of the storm on the Sea of Galilee. In the middle of that storm, Jesus said to the disciples, 'Where is your faith?'

As we go through storms and turbulent times, Jesus asks us the same question: 'Where is your faith?' You can't fool God. Either you mean what you pray or you don't. If you don't mean it, save your breath and don't pray. James' invitation is to single-minded devotion to God, praying to him for wisdom because we trust him. Let's pray to God in faith, trusting him, ready to be obedient to his will, not trying to bend him to ours.

Praying for wisdom will never be something we out-grow. We need wisdom more than ever to navigate our way through life in a way that pleases God. The Bible urges us to pursue wisdom relentlessly.

Do not forsake wisdom, and she will protect you;
    love her, and she will watch over you.
The beginning of wisdom is this: get wisdom.
    Though it cost all you have, get understanding.
(Proverbs 4:6–7)

Wisdom allows us to pursue what is good in life, not as judged by our standards, but as judged by the Creator. Wisdom allows us to see what is important to God, what values He gives us for our benefit, and it allows Him to teach us how we can pursue them.
(Tim Challies, *The Discipline of Spiritual Discernment*, Crossway, 2008, p. 56)

Day 29

Read: James 5:13–20
Key verse: James 5:13

· ·

Is anyone among you in trouble? Let them pray. Is anyone happy? Let them sing songs of praise.

When should we pray? James tells us to pray when we are 'in trouble' and when we are 'happy'.

First, pray when you are in trouble. The word for 'trouble' here conveys the idea of suffering evil. The same word is used in James 5:10 of the prophets who suffered persecution and in 2 Timothy 2:9 of suffering for the gospel, even to the point of being chained like a criminal. James' point is that when we endure hardship, we don't just sit with folded hands or engage in violent resistance; we pray. We pray for our enemies, our persecutors and for God's hand in the situation. We don't despair of the evil; we bring it to God. If your ministry or church is dealing with bitter opposition, then James urges you to start praying for those standing against you.

Second, we are to praise God when we are 'happy', although 'happy' is perhaps not the best translation. The original term really means 'in good heart': when Paul is shipwrecked in the middle of a raging storm, this is what he says (Acts 27:22, 25). He doesn't come up on deck to ask if people are happy. What he says is what James uses here: 'keep up your courage' or 'take heart' (ESV). Be of good heart, keep looking to God, although the storm rages round you, and sing praises. James is urging us to rejoice in God in all circumstances. We are not praising God *for* the evil. We are praising God because, in the worst evil, he is with us. Paul has the same message for us in 1 Thessalonians 5:16–18: 'Rejoice always, pray continually, give thanks in all circumstances; for this is God's will for you in Christ Jesus.'

Grant me more and more
    to prize the privilege of prayer,
    to come to thee as a sin-soiled sinner,
    to find pardon in thee,
    to converse with thee;
    to know thee in prayer as
        the path in which my feet tread,
        the latch upon the door of my lips,
        the light that shines through my eyes,

the music of my ears,
the marrow of my understanding,
the strength of my will,
the power of my affection,
the sweetness of my memory.
May the matter of my prayer be always
wise, humble, submissive,
obedient, scriptural, Christ-like.
Give me unwavering faith
that supplications are never in vain,
that if I seem not to obtain my petitions,
I shall have larger, richer answers,
surpassing all that I ask or think.
Unsought, thou hast given me
the greatest gift, the person of thy Son,
and in him thou wilt give me all I need.
(Arthur Bennett, 'The Prayer of Love', in *The Valley of Vision*, Banner of Truth Trust, 2002, pp. 270–271)

Day 30

Read: James 5:13–20
Key verse: James 5:14–16

....

> ¹⁴*Is anyone among you ill? Let them call the elders of the church to pray over them and anoint them with oil in the name of the Lord.* ¹⁵*And the prayer offered in faith will make the sick person well; the Lord will raise them up. If they have sinned, they will be forgiven.* ¹⁶*Therefore confess your sins to each other and pray for each other so that you may be healed. The prayer of a righteous person is powerful and effective.*

Is James saying that every time we pray for a sick person, he or she will be healed? We know from experience that God doesn't always work this way. So what do these verses mean?

Notice that the context of the whole chapter is the Lord's second coming, the end of life and meeting the Lord. We are not talking about ringing the pastor to come over because you have a sore throat. The reason the elders need to come to the patient's bedside is because the individual is too ill to go to church, literally 'at death's door'.

James says, 'The prayer offered in faith will make the sick person well.' The Greek word is actually 'save'. God may heal a person by bringing him or her back to full physical life or by saving the individual from the jaws of death. But he may also save someone by taking that person to be with him. This verse can mean both. Likewise, 'the Lord will raise them up' – he will raise the person up if there is physical healing, but he will also raise him or her up in the glorious resurrection. The role of the elders is to discern what God's will is. Is this a time when God will physically heal in a dramatic way or is this a moment when we sit, pray and read the Scriptures to a believer getting ready to meet the Lord? There are times when we sense God will heal and so we pray with confident faith because God has already given us extraordinary assurance. At other times, we leave a hospital bed knowing that we are on holy ground because a brother or sister has just walked into the presence of God.

The business of confession comes next because, when a person is preparing to pass into the presence of Jesus, it is important to know the assurance of the Lord's forgiveness. The interesting thing here is that, in verse 16, James uses the word 'healing'. Such is James the preacher: he uses 'saving' regarding sickness and 'healing' regarding confession because the full healing of God concerns the whole being. Healing is never to stand in the way of the full saving grace of the Lord because this body is going to be thrown away. The real person is eternal and will be for ever with the Lord.

Praying for the sick in your church is not solely the role of the elders. Today, pray that, if it is God's will, those who are unwell will be restored to full health. More importantly, pray for their spiritual healing. Pray for them to know the joy of their sins forgiven and to walk closely with God even in suffering.

For further study

If you would like to read more about prayer, you might find the following selection of books helpful:

- Alistair Begg, *Pray Big: Learn to Pray Like an Apostle* (Good Book Company, 2019).

- D. A. Carson, *A Call to Spiritual Reformation: Priorities from Paul and His Prayers* (IVP, 2011).

- Tim Chester, *You Can Pray* (IVP, 2014).

- Julian Hardyman, *Fresh Pathways in Prayer* (10Publishing, 2019).

- Tim Keller, *Prayer: Experiencing Awe and Intimacy with God* (Hodder & Stoughton, 2016).

- Paul E. Miller, *A Praying Life: Connecting with God in a Distracting World* (NavPress, 2017).

Keswick Ministries

Our purpose

Keswick Ministries exists to inspire and equip Christians to love and live for Christ in his world.

God's purpose is to bring his blessing to all the nations of the world (Genesis 12:3). That promise of blessing, which touches every aspect of human life, is ultimately fulfilled through the life, death, resurrection, ascension and future return of Christ. All of the people of God are called to participate in his missionary purposes, wherever he may place them. The central vision of Keswick Ministries is to see the people of God equipped, inspired and refreshed to fulfil that calling, directed and guided by God's Word in the power of his Spirit, for the glory of his Son.

Our priorities

There are three fundamental priorities which shape all that we do as we look to serve the local church.

- *Hearing God's Word*: the Scriptures are the foundation for the church's life, growth and mission, and Keswick Ministries is committed to preach and teach God's

Word in a way that is faithful to Scripture and relevant to Christians of all ages and backgrounds.

- *Becoming like God's Son*: from its earliest days, the Keswick movement has encouraged Christians to live godly lives in the power of the Spirit, to grow in Christ-likeness and to live under his lordship in every area of life. This is God's will for his people in every culture and generation.

- *Serving God's mission*: the authentic response to God's Word is obedience to his mission, and the inevitable result of Christlikeness is sacrificial service. Keswick Ministries seeks to encourage committed discipleship in family life, work and society, and energetic engagement in the cause of world mission.

Our ministry

- *Keswick Convention.* The Convention attracts some 12,000 to 15,000 Christians from the UK and around the world to Keswick every summer. It provides Bible teaching for all ages, vibrant worship, a sense of unity across generations and denominations, and an inspirational call to serve Christ in the world. It caters for children of all ages and has a strong youth and young adult programme. And it all takes place in the beautiful

Lake District – a perfect setting for rest, recreation and refreshment.

- *Keswick fellowship.* For more than 140 years, the work of Keswick has had an impact on churches worldwide, not just through individuals being changed but also through Bible conventions that originate or draw their inspiration from the Keswick Convention. Today, there is a network of events that shares Keswick Ministries' priorities across the UK and in many parts of Europe, Asia, North America, Australia, Africa and the Caribbean. Keswick Ministries is committed to strengthen the network in the UK and beyond, through prayer, news and cooperative activity.

- *Keswick teaching and training.* Keswick Ministries is developing a range of inspiring, equipping, Bible-centred teaching and training that focuses on 'whole-of-life' discipleship. This builds on the same concern that started the Convention: that all Christians live godly lives in the power of the Spirit in all spheres of life in God's world. Some of the events focus on equipping. They are smaller and more intensive. Others focus on inspiring. Some are for pastors, others for those in other forms of church leadership, while many are for any Christian. All courses aim to see participants return home refreshed to serve.

- *Keswick resources.* Keswick Ministries produces a range of books, devotionals and study guides as well as digital resources to inspire and equip Christians to live for Christ. The printed resources focus on the core foundations of Christian life and mission and help Christians in their walk with Christ. The digital resources make teaching and sung worship from the Keswick Convention available in a variety of ways.

Our unity

The Keswick movement worldwide has adopted a key Pauline statement to describe its gospel inclusivity: 'all one in Christ Jesus' (Galatians 3:28). Keswick Ministries works with evangelicals from a wide variety of church backgrounds, on the understanding that they share a commitment to the essential truths of the Christian faith as set out in our statement of belief.

Our contact details

T: 01768 780075
E: info@keswickministries.org
W: www.keswickministries.org
Mail: Keswick Ministries, Rawnsley Centre, Main Street, Keswick, Cumbria, CA12 5NP, England

Related titles from IVP

Food for the Journey

The Food for the Journey series offers daily devotionals from well-loved
Bible teachers at the Keswick Convention in an ideal pocket-sized format –
to accompany you wherever you go.

Available in the series

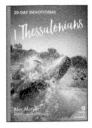 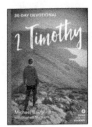  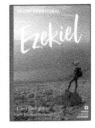

1 Thessalonians
Alec Motyer with
Elizabeth McQuoid
978 1 78359 439 9

2 Timothy
Michael Baughen with
Elizabeth McQuoid
978 1 78359 438 2

Colossians
Steve Brady with
Elizabeth McQuoid
978 1 78359 722 2

Ezekiel
Liam Goligher with
Elizabeth McQuoid
978 1 78359 603 4

   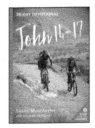

Habakkuk
Jonathan Lamb with
Elizabeth McQuoid
978 1 78359 652 2

Hebrews
Charles Price with
Elizabeth McQuoid
978 1 78359 611 9

James
Stuart Briscoe with
Elizabeth McQuoid
978 1 78359 523 5

John 14 - 17
Simon Manchester with
Elizabeth McQuoid
978 1 78359 495 5

Available from your local Christian bookshop or **www.ivpbooks.com**

Food for the Journey

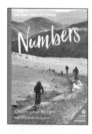

Numbers
Christopher Wright
with Elizabeth
McQuoid
978 1 78359 720 8

Revelation 1 - 3
Paul Mallard with
Elizabeth McQuoid
978 1 78359 712 3

Romans 5 - 8
John Stott with
Elizabeth McQuoid
978 1 78359 718 5

Ruth
Alistair Begg with
Elizabeth McQuoid
978 1 78359 525 9

Praise for the series

'This devotional series is biblically rich, theologically deep and full of wisdom . . . I recommend it highly.' **Becky Manley Pippert, speaker, author of** *Out of the Saltshaker and into the World* **and creator of the Live/Grow/ Know course and series of books**

'These devotional guides are excellent tools.' **John Risbridger, Minister and Team Leader, Above Bar Church, Southampton**

'These bite-sized banquets . . . reveal our loving Father weaving the loose and messy ends of our everyday lives into his beautiful, eternal purposes in Christ.' **Derek Burnside, Principal, Capernwray Bible School**

'I would highly recommend this series of 30-day devotional books to anyone seeking a tool that will help [him or her] to gain a greater love of scripture, or just simply . . . to do something out of devotion. Whatever your motivation, these little books are a must-read.' **Claud Jackson,** *Youthwork* **Magazine**

Available from your local Christian bookshop or **www.ivpbooks.com**

Related teaching CD and DVD packs

CD PACKS

1 Thessalonians
SWP2203D (5-CD pack)

2 Timothy
SWP2202D (4-CD pack)

Colossians
SWP2318D (4-CD pack)

Ezekiel
SWP2263D (5-CD pack)

Habakkuk
SWP2299D (5-CD pack)

Hebrews
SWP2281D (5-CD pack)

James
SWP2239D (4-CD pack)

John 14 - 17
SWP2238D (5-CD pack)

Numbers
SWP2317D (5-CD pack)

Revelation
SWP2300D (5-CD pack)

Romans 5 - 8
SWP2316D (4-CD pack)

Ruth
SWP2280D (5-CD pack)

Available from www.essentialchristian.com

Related teaching CD and DVD packs

DVD PACKS

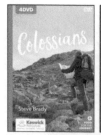   

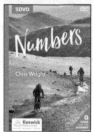  

Colossians
SWP2318A (4-DVD pack)

Ezekiel
SWP2263A (5-DVD pack)

Habakkuk
SWP2299A (5-DVD pack)

John 14 - 17
SWP2238A (5-DVD pack)

Numbers
SWP2317A (5-DVD pack)

Revelation
SWP2300A (5-DVD pack)

Ruth
SWP2280A (5-DVD pack)

Food for the Journey THEMES

The Food for the Journey: Themes offers daily devotions from well-loved Bible teachers at the Keswick Convention, exploring how particular themes are woven through the Bible and what we can learn from them today. In a convenient, pocket-sized format, these little books are ideal to accompany you wherever you go.

Available in the series

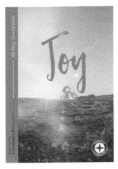

Joy
Elizabeth McQuoid
978 1 78974 163 6

Persevere
Elizabeth McQuoid
978 1 78974 102 5

Pray
Elizabeth McQuoid
978 1 78974 169 8

'A rich feast! . . . We can still have joy in Jesus, even when there are tears in our eyes.'
Edrie Mallard

'I have had the JOY of reading this book in advance and I am excited.'
George Verwer

'Packed full of essential theology, especially important when the going gets tough . . . There's no "junk" here. It's all "food", essential for our walk with God, whatever the terrain.'
Catherine Campbell

'The ideal reboot for a flagging devotional life . . . warm and biblical practical.'
Julian Hardyman

'What a great way to spend a month, studying prayer with such a wide range of applications.'
Karen Soole

Available from your local Christian bookshop or **www.ivpbooks.com**